DIGITAL CAREER

CAREER

CREATING MOBILE APPS

ERIN STALEY

D1070383

ROSEN
PUBLISHING
New York

Published in 2014 by The Rosen Publishing Group, Inc.
29 East 21st Street, New York, NY 10010

Library of Congress Cataloging-in-Publication Data

Staley, Erin.
Career building through creating mobile apps/Erin Staley. — First edition.
        pages cm — (Digital career building)
Includes bibliographical references and index.
Audience: Grades 7-12.
ISBN 978-1-4777-1727-1 (library binding) — ISBN 978-1-4777-1737-0 (pbk.) —
ISBN 978-1-4777-1738-7 (6-pack)
1. Mobile computing—Vocational guidance—Juvenile literature.
2. Smartphones—Programming—Vocational guidance—Juvenile
literature. 3. Application software—Development—Vocational
guidance—Juvenile literature. I. Title.
QA76.59.S73 2013
004.023—dc23

                                                                    2013020100

Manufactured in the United States of America

CPSIA Compliance Information: Batch #W14YA: For further information, contact Rosen Publishing, New
York, New York, at 1-800-237-9932.

CONTENTS

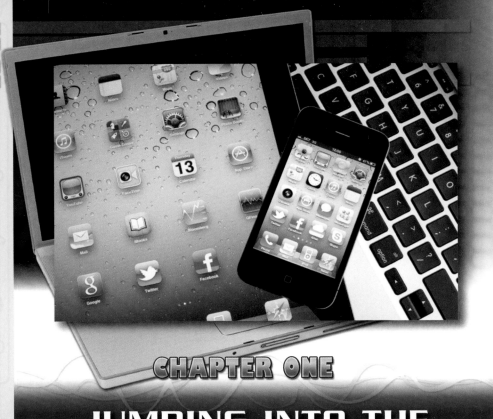

CHAPTER ONE

JUMPING INTO THE DIGITAL APP WORLD

From mowing lawns to babysitting, from lifeguarding to delivering pizza, entrepreneurial teens have worked all sorts of odd jobs to raise a little extra cash. However, the world has become more hi-tech. Savvy teens are turning their tech hobbies into money-making enterprises. In addition, they are using these experiences as a springboard for college applications and promising careers in digital communications.

What Is an App?

Often called an "app," a mobile application is an individual software unit used to add specific functionality to mobile devices, such as computers, tablets, and smartphones. While an app has limited capabilities, it offers

JUMPING INTO THE DIGITAL APP WORLD

 There is a rising number of self-taught teen developers who are making an impressive impact on the app development industry. Their creations are fresh and profitable, inspiring other teens in this new mobile app economy.

capabilities that can entertain with games and videos or share information such as news, weather, and financial reports. Whether you want to snap a picture of your cross-country road trip, save your most important passwords, learn a new language, or find out which team won the season final, these power-packed software units will place the world at your fingertips.

 According to Kristin Marino's article "How to Become a Mobile App Developer," among the most popular apps are games (64 percent of users who download), weather (60 percent), social networking (56 percent), maps/navigation/search (51 percent), and music (44 percent).

A History of Apps

When the first mobile phone, the Motorola DynaTAC 8000X, was introduced to consumers in 1983, it was nothing like the high-tech smartphones of today. It weighed 1 kilogram (2.2 pounds), stored up to thirty phone numbers, offered only one hour of battery life, and cost almost $4,000. In 1997, Nokia embedded *Snake* in to its 6610 mobile phone. A remake of the 1970s' computer game, the pixilated reptile grew as it slid through a tiny maze detailed against a green background. Although pretty basic by today's standards, *Snake* was a hit with users. Its success inspired other companies to add arcade-like games to their mobile devices, including *Pong, Tic-Tac-Toe*, and *Tetris*. They also began adding productivity apps, including calculators, calendars, e-mail capabilities, and ringtones. Just about every mobile phone blasted the chorus of a top 40 hit in the late 1990s and early 2000s.

Competition was fierce among mobile service providers, and trade secrets were closely guarded. Mobile apps could only be created by in-house designers. The development of Wireless Application Protocol (WAP)—a similar version of HTTP—was what third-party developers needed to get their foot in the door. WAP allowed minimalized Web pages to be easily displayed on very small screens or feed apps with live content to mobile devices using a wireless network. It was supported by all operating systems and worked within the memory and bandwidth limitations of many mobile devices. With a WAP access point on the device, the third-party

 The 1973 DynaTAC prototype (*left*) was the first portable cellular phone. The 1984 Motorola DynaTAC 8000X (*right*) was the world's first commercially available portable cellular phone.

developers were free to create new and exciting content to the amazement of users. Yet WAP had its disadvantages. Downloading efforts were sluggish, and data transfer was an expensive luxury. Developers had difficulty adapting their content because of display and interactivity limitations. In the end, third-party developers were unsuccessful in creating effective apps. Still, developers knew mobile app development would become a gold mine. Platforms began offering ports for discovery, purchasing, and installation, and the user interface (UI) standards changed completely. Developers kept pushing through, and soon, mobile phone capabilities were limitless.

Apple understood this shift and saw an opportunity to provide third-party developers with a digital opportunity. In October 2007, Steve Jobs of Apple declared that the iPhone would open up to third-party developers the following year. This meant the app market was wide open for anyone to step in and create a piece of digital history. Because development costs were low, designers jumped at the chance to be a part of the digital app world. It seemed as if the development track from hardware to software boomed overnight, but it did take time for Apple to merge the technical and business aspects of its vision. However, both elements came together, and in 2008, Apple launched its App Store. Five hundred apps filled the pages, and customers couldn't get enough of them. The mobile app phenomenon had officially begun. As smartphones became more sophisticated—and e-readers, iPads, iPods, and tablets entered the market— customers demanded apps that were easy to find and install. New app stores hit the market, happy to offer a

MAKING APP STORE HISTORY

Where does one go for the latest in mobile apps? Why the app store, of course. Users can simply access their mobile device's app store and shop among the thousands of entertainment, social media, business, and news apps. With the tap of a button, they can view app photos and reviews as well as various price points. The first app store to make history was the legendary Apple App Store. It opened in July 2008, and within one week, ten million mobile apps were downloaded. Only 25 percent of these were free, meaning that customers were happy to pay for apps that customized their devices.

The Apple App Store paved the way for others to hit the market. The Android Market opened its virtual doors in 2008, followed by the Ovi Store in 2009, BB App World in 2009, and Windows Phone Marketplace in 2010. Today, the Apple App Store sells thousands of mobile apps for the iPhone, iPad, and iPod Touch. In fact, it reached twenty-five billion downloads in the spring of 2012.

The mobile app market is an independent developer's digital dream. Developers can create and code innovative mobile apps while relying on the app store to handle the business side of selling apps. For a cut of the profits—usually 30 percent—an app store will cover marketing and sales distribution. This frees the developer to become a digital superstar with his or her creative ideas, attractive content, and proper implementation.

wide variety of free or affordably priced apps compatible with other operating systems, such as Android, BlackBerry OS, Windows Phone OS, and iOS. Each operating system required the application to be written

entirely from scratch in the compatible operating system's language. This meant that developers needed a working knowledge of specific coding languages, such as Java for Android and BlackBerry, C++ for Windows Mobile, and Objective-C for iOS.

Types of Apps

Along with numerous programming languages, there are three types of mobile aps: native, mobile Web, and hybrid. The native app is a standalone app created specifically for the operating system of a mobile device. Most mobile games are native apps, such as *Cut the Rope*, *Plants vs. Zombies*, and the mega hit *Angry Birds*. A native app must be downloaded from an app store. App developers who wish to create native apps have the benefit of standardized software development kits (SDKs). Provided by the platform manufacturer, SDKs include user interface elements and development tools. While native apps are fast and are often kept up to date, they are expensive to build and maintain. Examples include *Camera+* for devices using the iOS operating system or *KeePassDroid* for Android devices.

Mobile Web apps are Web-based and are compatible with other mobile platforms. These apps do not need to be downloaded from a traditional app store. They are simply accessed from within the device's Web browser. Examples include *Instagram*, *DropBox*, *Google Maps*, and *YouTube*. Developers who want to create mobile Web apps can use some of the server-side languages, Web application frameworks, or computer programming code—HTML5, CSS3, or JavaScript—they may already

A *Plants vs. Zombies* character is photographed at E3 2012's Namco Bandai booth in Los Angeles. *Plants vs. Zombies* is a video game phenomenon that can be played on most mobile devices and game stations.

know. They are not required to use SDKs and can avoid the approval process required by app stores altogether. Because mobile Web apps are less expensive to produce, they are more affordable. Users love mobile Web apps

because the source of each app updates them on a regular basis. However, it is important to note that the offline data storage is limited, and mobile Web apps sometimes lack the refined design of native apps. In addition, it can be tricky to get these apps to work properly with the numerous browsers available to smartphone users.

Hybrid apps bring together Web technology and native app execution. Hybrid apps such as Facebook, LinkedIn, and TuneIn Radio combine the convenience of HTML5, CSS, or Javascript Web apps within a native mobile framework. This allows the user to have a mobile Web browser functioning within the app. Hybrid apps can be downloaded from an app store and are used across multiple mobile platforms. Users download the app framework specifically for their platform, and the content will be provided through platform independent online channels. Hybrid apps are even accessible when the device is offline. Many retailers prefer hybrid apps. Customers activate their native app on their mobile device when shopping but go through Web-generated information when checking out.

Today, the app craze shows no signs of stopping. An International Data Corporation (IDC) report from December 2010 notes that "global downloads will reach 76.9 billion in 2014 and will be worth US$35 billion." A Canalys report from June 2011 agrees, predicting that "direct revenue from the sale of apps, in-app purchases, and subscriptions across smartphones and tablets" will reach $36.7 billion in 2015. Mobile app development is a thriving business, and developers, including digital-savvy teens, are rising to the challenge. Many of these teens were able to make a living long before they passed a driving test or earned their high school diploma. They turned their hobbies into profits, moving beyond the mundane and venturing into this ever-changing digital market of mobile apps. Are you ready to do the same? Are you ready to jump into the digital world with mobile app development?

It's a prime time to get involved in mobile app development. According to PricewaterhouseCoopers, the global wireless games market will reach $12.7 billion by 2014.

CHAPTER TWO

APPRENEURS MAKE MOBILE APP RICHES

Compared to other professions, mobile app development is relatively new. This means that top developers may not have formal developer backgrounds. Some come with a long list of credentials and achievements in related fields. As an ATM software designer, Steve Demeter took to designing apps in his spare time. He had been inspired by attending an iPhone conference in the summer of 2007. He believed Apple was opening a world of opportunity to developers when it released the SDK. This allowed third-party apps to be downloaded onto mobile devices, and Demeter knew his experience could open the door for him into the budding industry.

 Steve Demeter arrives at the Academy of Interactive Arts and Sciences' 12th Annual Interactive Achievement Awards in Las Vegas, Nevada. The AIAS honors those who have made outstanding achievements in the video game industry.

He spent months brainstorming a clever, yet original, game app. In February 2008, he had his idea. After four months of tirelessly coding on evenings and weekends, *Trism* was ready for its 2008 debut in Apple's App Store. Within the first two months, Demeter earned $250,000 with his brightly colored triangle game. He eventually quit his bank job and launched Demiforce, a game development company.

Some top developers have taught themselves the art and science of building apps using online tools. Not only does the Internet offer the marketplace, but it contains the main information source and training camp. Written or even animated tutorials are available for almost any step of app development. Thousands of forums and networks dedicate themselves to app development. Chad Mureta, a self-taught app developer, was introduced to the mobile app industry in quite a different manner. In 2009, Mureta flipped his car and severely injured his dominant arm. He was laid up in the hospital for weeks. During the lengthy recovery, a friend gave him an article about app-making entrepreneurs called "appreneurs." Most were one- or two-person teams developing apps. Their start-up costs were low, and Mureta learned that the successful appreneurs were making thousands, if not millions, of dollars with their designs. Inspired to get involved, Mureta began developing apps from his hospital bed. He believed this business opportunity would help him pay his staggering medical bills. After eighteen months of rehab, and endless hours developing apps, Mureta was able to leave his real estate company. He replaced his seventy-hour workweek with a five-hour

BUSINESSES AND MOBILE APP DEVELOPMENT

Businesses are always looking for ways to improve their operations, increase productivity, and bring in more profits. Mobile apps are a promising way to achieve these goals. Everyone from international fashion houses to vehicle rental agencies has added mobile apps to their marketing strategies as a part of branding.

In the past, only established corporations maximized the benefits of mobile apps. That is not the case today. Businesses of all sizes now generate apps for sale or distribution. For instance, a local wedding planner may use an app to help clients plan their special day. Or a delivery service will create an app to help customers track packages sent to loved ones around the world. In addition, entrepreneurs and associates can perform in-house tasks by using company apps. They can manage inventory, access customer databases, and complete timecards within minutes, even seconds. Businesses can use apps to generate income. Many entrepreneurs choose to sell a premium mobile app version to those who desire an upgrade from their free app. Others offer advertising or listings to be displayed within the app itself. For example, a publishing company may pay a local bookstore to include its catalog in the bookstore's app. A wealth of options awaits savvy business owners who recognize the benefits and advantages of the mobile app industry.

App makers interested in developing a mobile app for a business must understand the company's challenges and expectations. What does the organization want to accomplish? How can it reach out to new and existing clients? Once the app developer has an understanding of the business's objectives, he or she can create an app. With a polished app on their mobile devices, users can pay a bill, fill a prescription, or plan a vacation to sunny Mexico.

work week, working anywhere in the world from his iPhone as an appreneur. Tim Ferriss quotes Mureta on FourHourWorkWeek.com:

> In just over two years, I've created and sold three app companies that have generated millions in revenue. Two months after launching my first company, one of my apps averaged $30,000 a month in profit. In December of 2010, the company's monthly income had reached $120,000. In all, I've developed more than forty apps and have had more than thirty-five million app downloads across the globe. Over 90 percent of my apps were successful and made money.

Nick D'Aloisio

Whiz kids are jumping into the app development industry, too. Nick D'Aloisio has always been drawn to technology. When he was eight years old, his parents bought him an iPod. The next year, he begged them for a Mac. Nick used his new desktop computer to make films and eventually moved on to programming—Final Cut, Final Cut Pro, and 3D-rendering software—when Apple opened its App Store. Nick was only twelve years old.

He developed a number of apps, including *Fingermill*, *Facemood*, and *SongStumblr*. While studying for history labs, fifteen-year-old Nick discovered the inefficiencies of popular search engines. He got to work developing something better. From his makeshift bedroom-app development control center, he developed an algorithm for his new iOS app. The app was called *Trimit*, and it summarized magazine and newspaper articles, giving readers the gist on a single smartphone screen. The app was launched in November 2012, and it was a hit with more than two hundred thousand users. *Summly* won the title of one of Apple's best apps that same year. Nick's savvy app caught the attention of Li Ka-shing and his venture capital firm, Horizon Ventures. The Hong Kong billionaire invested $300,000 and was joined by other investors, including Ashton Kutcher; Yoko Ono; Stephen Fry; Joanna Shields, the head of London's Tech City; and Zynga founder Marc Pincus.

    Summly was a hit with international news organizations. They appreciated the additional traffic to their Web sites. Some of these organizations struck a deal to highlight their publications within the app. Depending on where the reader is in the world, he or she will receive

At seventeen, Nick D'Aloisio made headlines around the world when he sold his mega hit, *Summly*, to Yahoo!. His hard work and ingenuity has inspired fellow teens to try their hand at becoming successful appreneurs.

one of News Corporation's local publications. If the reader is in the United States, he or she will read the *Wall Street Journal*; in England, *The Times of London*; in Australia, *The Australian*. In March 2013, Yahoo! acquired *Summly* for $30 million. *Summly* will close as it is and be incorporated into Yahoo!'s mobile experiences. Nick will go to work in Yahoo!'s London offices while he finishes his schooling. This remarkable opportunity opens up a world of mobile opportunities for developers of all ages.

Thomas Suarez

Like Nick D'Aloisio, Thomas Suarez was fascinated by computers and technology. As a twelve year old, he was known as the youngest iPhone app developer, creating apps for the iPhone, iPod touch, and iPad. He mastered programming languages such as Python, C, and Java while the SDK allowed him to design apps, one of which was *Earth Fortune*. He persuaded his parents, Ralph and Margaret, to pay $99 to get his app on Apple's App Store. Thomas created *Bustin Jieber*, a whack-a-mole game using Justin Bieber heads. He got the idea because so many of his classmates disliked the famous Canadian singer. It was released just before the holidays in 2010 and sold for 99 cents. To date, this is Thomas's most successful—and most favorite—mobile app. He started CarrotCorp, a company that sold four mobile apps using the iOS platform.

In October 2011, Thomas spoke at the TedxManhattanBeach event in California. The title of his presentation was "Thomas Suarez: A 12-Year-Old App

Craig Hatkoff (*left*) and Thomas Suarez (*right*) onstage at the Tribeca Disruptive Innovative Awards ceremony during the 2012 Tribeca Film Festival in New York City.

Developer." He shared that while many kids like to play mobile games, they also want to learn how to create the apps. They simply do not know how to get started in the relatively new industry. During Thomas's Tedx presentation, Craig Hatkoff, the cofounder of the Tribeca Film Festival, was inspired by Thomas's insight. He decided to mentor Thomas, and bought the young developer a MakerBot 3D. This desktop replicator allows designers to design and print three-dimensional objects. It became

one of Thomas's favorite tools. Thomas was one of the honored guests at the 2012 Tribeca Disruptive Innovation Awards. At the event, Hatkoff gave Thomas a "Disruptive Innovation" award in the shape of a hammer. Hatkoff told Abby Ellin and Joanna Stern of ABCNews.go.com, "I started off thinking Thomas would become my protégé. I have now learned, I am his protégé." In turn, Thomas gave Hatkoff his MakerBot creation. To help his peers interested in developing apps, Thomas started an app club at his school. It is here where students can network, sharing ideas and support.

WATCH OUT Many people are joining the app craze with a get-rich-quick mentality and unrealistic expectations. Maintaining an optimistic perspective is important, but so is understanding that you will have to put in work. Very few app developers strike it rich overnight. It takes time, patience, experience, and a willingness to make changes when needed.

Spencer Costanzo

Spencer Costanzo, another teen appreneur, started Malibu Apps while he was in high school. The company offers iPhone and Android app development consultations, as well as app icon design, graphic design, and e-book publishing services. Spencer got his start when he released his first app in June 2011. It grossed only $10 a day in the App Store. Spencer decided to release a second mobile app. Only this time, it contained half the content of the original app. This second attempt earned $25 a day.

Spencer experimented by doubling the price. Within twenty-four hours, the app grossed $40 a day, and for every day after, Spencer's app brought in $100 to $150 per day. Although the apps were removed for copywriting infringement, Spencer was hooked. During a two-week vacation in 2011, he worked in the hotel's business center, developing and releasing two more apps. Sales from these made it more than worth his time and efforts. Spencer told Kara Ohngren of YoungEntreprenuer.com:

> Not many people know how to create profitable iPhone apps, so I had to test, make changes, test again, make more changes and test fifty more times. I'm still testing new strategies today. When you're creating apps through outsourcing, the process includes coming up with great app ideas, finding highly skilled employees, diagramming how your app will function, marketing, and coordinating the entire process.

Malibu Apps was awarded Young Entrepreneur's Startup of the Month for October 2012. Since its inception, Malibu Apps has released over fifty apps, including *10-Step Nutrition Program to Master Healthy Living*, *Complete Guide to Minecraft*, *My Best Dog Breed*, and *All Golden Eggs* for *Angry Birds Seasons*. Spencer had intended to take a year off and enter college in 2013. However, his net income quickly exceeded $100,000 before the end of the first fiscal year. He and his parents began to think that college might not be the best route.

They supported his decision to continue building Malibu Apps and Malibu Microcap LLC, a company that invests and advises start-up app companies. Today, Spencer's philosophy, "Build your own dream, or someone will hire you to build theirs," is the backbone of his entrepreneurial efforts. When asked about sharing advice for aspiring young entrepreneurs, Spender told YoungEntreprenuer.com:

> If someone tells you your business idea is crazy, you're probably onto something. Most people aren't innovative and think inside the box. While this is the safe thing to do, great things are always the result of thinking differently. You'll never know if it was a bad idea until you try it. If my first few apps hadn't completely failed, I would never have known what to do differently to create a successful app business.

 At nine years old, Thomas Suarez downloaded the iOS Developer ToolKit and simulation tool onto his computer. He used this to teach himself Python, Java, and C.

CHAPTER THREE

ON YOUR MARK, GET SET...

If you're obsessed with the idea of turning your hobby into a paycheck, now is the time to jump into the industry. There is no time to waste to get a piece of the pie. Neil Parmar of YoungEntrepreneur.com wrote, "Even if you took the market value of all of the goods and services that are produced annually across Aruba, Fiji, Barbados, Grenada and Greenland, you'd still fall short of the global revenues that were generated last year [2011] through mobile apps: $15.1 billion." That's a sizable pie, and you can have a piece of it.

While it may be tempting to count the thousands of dollars to be earned, there are often many sacrifices to be made when taking on a new adventure. Are you

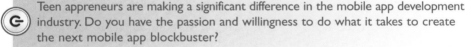
Teen appreneurs are making a significant difference in the mobile app development industry. Do you have the passion and willingness to do what it takes to create the next mobile app blockbuster?

ready to dedicate every free moment to app development, even if it means staying up until the wee hours of the morning to finish creating your one-of-a-kind app? Are you willing to skip parties, dates, club meetings, and the Friday-night game to develop a top app in your favorite app store? Are you so obsessed with app development that you'll scrape, together every last cent to invest in educational tools, equipment, or a development team?

OUTSOURCING

Simple apps can be designed with minimal assistance, but more sophisticated apps may need a little extra help. If you find your skill set to be lacking, you could hire a freelancer to breathe life into your vision. Finding the right person or team to help you create an app is no small task. It's important to ask for referrals and work samples before engaging in any contractual agreement. Be clear when you describe your project to the freelancer and list your expectations. Define the platform you prefer, as well as the expectations you have before moving forward. Be sure to determine their strengths, weaknesses, and quickness to respond to communications. Friends and family can often give feedback during the development process. Safeguard your project by requesting a signed confidentially agreement before any work is completed. This can include project details, expectations, and terms of payment. Also, request the source code—the programming language text intended for a computer program. You may need this information if you need to part ways with your current development company and employ another team.

Third-party developers charge a fee depending on the type of app and its level of sophistication. One-function apps such as *Notes* and *Calculators* can cost anywhere from $500 to $10,000. More complicated apps with multiple graphics and screens can cost up to $200,000. These can include city guides, videos, and e-commerce apps. The costs and challenges of creating multiple or cross-platform developing can be quite complicated. Many independent developers are not familiar with numerous mobile operating systems and programming languages. Third-party developers can help port your creation to other systems.

QUICK TIP

If you are a beginner, have your idea evaluated by an expert. He or she can be a developer, marketer, or social media professional with experience in launching mobile apps. This expert will be able to give you honest feedback and suggestions to make it better.

Cameron Oelsen and Antony Basta are two teen developers who decided to build their technological dreams despite a busy high school workload and social life. The two met at A. E. Wright Middle School in Calabasas, California, and shared a common interest in Web site design. By the time they were seventeen years old, they were developing iPhone and iPad apps. Their

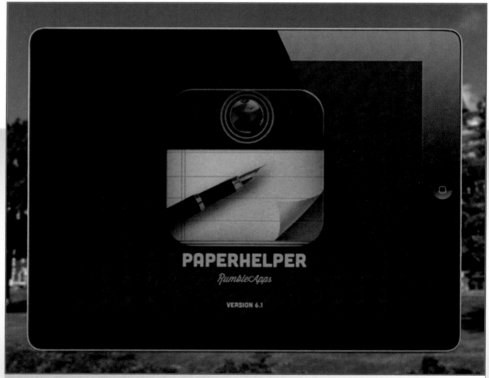

PaperHelper, the iPad app featuring a side-by-side browser and document writer, solved the problem of switching screens to complete an assignment. Do you have a solution-minded idea for an ingenious mobile app?

first was *QuikSocial*, allowing users to simultaneously accesses social networks. Later apps included *BloodPressurePro*, which offers blood pressure readings, and *PaperHelper*, which splits the iPad screen into two displays—one for a document and the other for an Internet browser. In 2010, Cameron and Antony started their own company, RumbleApps. They run it just like other successful business executives. Customer service issues are handled during school breaks, while meetings and ongoing projects are reserved for late hours: 9 PM to 2 AM.

Mapping Your Goals

If you think you're ready to take on the challenges of mobile app development, then it's time to roll up your sleeves and map out your goals. What do you want to build? Who are you building it for? Apps directly target a particular audience, so you need to know your target market. For example, children like games, while their parents would prefer their children have games with an educational element. Teens, the highest app downloaders, tend to select trendy apps that involve music, videos, dating advice, fashion, and Hollywood updates. The adult market can vary depending on age and interest. As the planning continues, ask yourself, "Why will they want to use my app?" and "What makes it unique?" Perform in-depth market research before you begin developing. You may notice that social media and game apps tend to top app store lists in every platform. Puzzles, educational learning, and e-commerce apps are also well received. Many successful app developers download popular apps

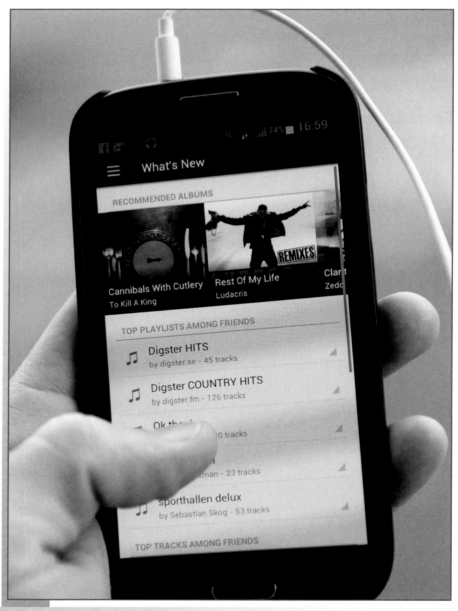

Android app *Spotify* is a Swedish music streaming service that allows users to share their favorite tunes. Browse your way through millions of tracks and discover new favorites with instant recommendations.

that have made an impact on the market. They study the user interface, looking for ways to tap into the wish lists of potential users.

There are a number of technical skills needed to develop mobile apps. You may need to understand the functionality of the device's operating system and answer with the appropriate computing skills, such as database management, memory allocation, security, and hardware interaction. Classic object-oriented programming languages such as Java and C++ are a must. Mobile platform APIs—Apple iOS, Android, BlackBerry, and Windows Mobile—are the core of knowledge along with understanding the platform's SDK. Web development languages such as HTML, CSS, Javascript, or even PHP, PERL and ASP are invaluable. Then there are the cross-platform mobile suites of Antenna and AMP. You may face a big challenge if you decide to cross-platform formatting, and then build what should be built according to that mobile's functionality. Cross-platform formatting is making an application compatible for different mobile operating systems.

Although it may seem overwhelming, many developers choose to delegate the technical responsibility to others. You can act as a project manager, overseeing the stages of the project. Find others who have been successful in the business and learn from them. Learn from their process and emulate their model. Expert developers say that if you can draw your idea on a piece of paper, you can build an app. Once you have a planning strategy in place, it's time to draft a technical design mock-up.

Julien Beasley (*right*), a graphics processing unit design lead from Advanced Micro Devices, competes in a "hackathon," a development event. Peter Dwersteg (*left*), a Microsoft Windows 8 operating system developer, offers collaboration.

How will your app work? Storyboard mock-ups allow you to test before you code, saving time and money in the long run. As mentioned earlier, there are a number of technological skills that will help you become a well-rounded developer. If you are planning to develop an app from scratch, it's important to note that it is not an easy path to take. Along with technical skills, app development requires listening to others, time management, flexibility, and planning. The best way to fast forward your process is to set short- and long-term goals. All you need is one amazing idea. If it's well executed, it can change the app world. If your idea is catchy and convenient and works well within the platform and marketplace, then it's time to put it into action. Are you willing to jump into the wonderful world of mobile app development?

WATCH OUT Intellectual property refers to literary and artistic branding and content used in commerce. There are laws in place to protect one's intellectual property. You can avoid legal complications—and high legal costs—by researching your genre before creating an app.

CHAPTER FOUR

...DEVELOP!

It's important to know that there isn't a magical spell or fail-proof formula for app development. Depending on enthusiasm, skill level, and resources, it may take anywhere from a few hours to several months to develop the first draft of your app. From there, you'll likely experience many rounds of trial and error before reaching notable achievement. Most app developers fail before they succeed. Take for instance the developer company that created the most popular mobile app game of all time, *Angry Birds*. It was Rovio's fifty-second game app, proving that developing successful apps is all about never giving up.

 Designed by Rovio Entertainment Oy, *Angry Birds* became a worldwide phenomenon within a few months of its release. It is the top-paid app of all time.

 To convey your idea properly, simply draw it on a piece of paper. Some developers use Photoshop's Draft or Finger Print Security Pro.

Quality is number one when it comes to app development. You will want to design an app that grabs the user's attention within ten to fifteen seconds. It needs to be user-friendly, attractive, and speedy. People always look for good applications, but you will want to be sure your app works and is of high quality. Avoid tripping up your user with too many "bells and whistles" that can complicate the design, speed, and consistency of your app. Consider a

SUBMITTING YOUR APP

Submitting your app to an app store can take anywhere from one to two weeks. Each store has its own requirements regarding mobile platforms and operating systems, and some are stricter than others. App store representatives review thousands of apps each week. They consider the overall customer experience, knowing this is the key to their success. Reviewers take into account the quality, overall functionality, release date, and firmware requirement. They want to avoid users downloading the app only to discover their devices were not technically capable of using the app. Most app stores have no tolerance for obscenity or applications that will damage mobile devices.

Developers benefit when their apps are listed with an app store. Not only do they have exposure to an international market, app stores also offer free analytic tools for further insight. Developers can look at downloading times to determine strategic time frames for future marketing efforts. Also, app stores provide geographic information, disclosing users' locations when downloading an app. This will benefit your future marketing and product efforts.

App developers are not limited to app stores, however. They can use independent app stores like GetJar. Founded in Lithuania, GetJar is an independent mobile phone app store and the largest free app store in the world. It provides over 150,000 apps for all sorts of platforms. GetJar gives free rewards to users for trying new apps. This could entice more users to access your new app. The most important key is to submit your high-quality app. The more locations you submit to, the better your chance of reaching users who will want to download your creation.

separate app for each task to offer the specific functionality in the best possible way. Less is more.

With a workable version of your app, be sure to have it tested by a group of objective representatives from your target market. Most seasoned app developers recommend a minimum of three user test rounds per release. Observe their interaction with your prototype. Is the app quick enough when given a command? Do the functions work? Or does an error message pop up? Interview the testers by asking them what they are thinking as they use the app. What are they expecting it to do for them? Welcome feedback, especially those notes that call for improvements. Then prioritize error corrections and enhancements. Some improvements can wait for the second version of the app.

Setting a Price Point

Now that your shiny new app has been tested, it's time to consider the price point. A majority of apps are free, while many are between 99 cents and $5. Specialized apps can sell for hundreds or thousands of dollars. These include a $300 piano tuner app, a $900 video surveillance app, or a $1,000 study guide for lawyers wanting to pass the California bar exam. Specialized apps are the exception, as they all have clearly defined market values and limited audiences.

Begin your app development journey with free or "lite" version apps. By discovering users' reactions to functionality and design, you will gain valuable knowledge for future projects. Plus, free apps tend to generate the

Pandora is just one mobile app that you can download. The number of musical apps is vast, so you are sure to never be without music.

most traffic. They are quick to download, and most users find it difficult to resist a free puzzle, recipe page, or talking cartoon. Although an app is free, developers can still make money on the app. How? They use in-app advertising. Some even gather personal data to sell to other companies. Developers hope users are so taken with the free app that they will purchase the upgraded version when the "nag screens" pop up. A percentage of users will buy the paid or "pro" version just to avoid advertising interruptions. Some app developers choose to set up a subscription model, distributing valuable information to paying users. Regardless of the options you choose, keep in mind that quality matters most when one is working to gain customer loyalty and referrals.

Monetization partners can help maximize revenue from your mobile apps with in-app advertising. One such monetization partner is Google's AdMob. Developers can choose from thousands of advertisers, selecting those that enhance their app. Payment is

received when an ad is clicked by a user. As you launch your app, you could see money hit your bank account within two months.

Take some time to think about the branding of your app. It will give your creation a professional and distinctive presence in the market. Branding starts with a name and extends to design, colors, fonts, music, and copywriting. Successful developers recommend looking at competitors within your genre. How are they presenting their apps in the market? Then look at your own branding. How can you use what you've learned for your overall design? Next comes the marketing with app store promotions, social media campaigns, and launch parties. Keep in mind that different target audiences require different types of marketing. Advertising to teenagers is different from advertising to retirees. It may take a good week or a few months to hone in on a marketing campaign. But let's face it, not every remarkable programmer excels at marketing. A reliable and equally impassioned partner with whom to share these responsibilities may be needed.

If you are lacking advertising funds and choose to market your app as a developer, be innovative. This is the time to explain the purpose of the app. Build relationships with your audience before you release the new app. Securing several dozens of good reviews in app stores by the first day will entice others to click the "purchase" button. Also, include snappy product descriptions. Take advantage of free resources, such as Facebook fan pages, Twitter, YouTube, and blogs. Send out daily reminders, breaking news, and requests for reviews and ratings. If your app is fun and unique, your online friends will use it and share it with others, helping to build a community of fans. Experiment with multiple channels to see what works, but whatever you do, don't stop promoting your app. If you have a high-quality app, users will be passionate and recommend it to others. Soon the app will sell itself.

Monitoring your app's online buzz is key to your success. Analytics will help you determine the success of your app by noting the number of downloads, unique users, page views, and session length. You can invest in internal analytics to discover user values, customer attribution models, and monetization payouts. External analytic tools such as *App Annie* or *Distimo* will help you decide which market and platforms you want to target. In addition, app stores offer ratings and reviews while Facebook's Insight displays user activity reports, post activity, and demographics within your Facebook community. A keyword search will determine which sites promote your mobile app. If something isn't working, change it.

Once your app has been launched, there will be some "bug fixing" and maintenance to handle. Your reviewers will tell you what is working and what isn't. Answer their concerns quickly and professionally, as good service will always impact your future sales. Also, consider updating your app in the future. Perhaps it needs a new eye-catching design, improved user involvement, additional features, or more competitive pricing. This could take up to a minute for a quick modification or several months for a complete overhaul.

CREATING MOBILE APPS

Even highly popular apps have short shelf lives when it comes to sales. There is quite a lot of movement on app charts. This means that users have to be engaged with updated versions.

As the world of app development continues to open up to you, remember to take one step at a time. If ideas flood your mind, select just one to develop. Successful developers make notes of app ideas that jump into their heads but discipline themselves to the one app they're working on at the moment. By methodically setting short- and long-term goals, you can be well on your way to generating money and even a long-term career. Who knows? You may create the next *Draw Something*, downloaded 50 million times before being purchased for a reported $200 million by Zynga, or *Instagram*, which was

Instagram transforms the look of photos and allows users to share them online. In 2013, Instagram began offering a movie camera icon. Users can create and post fifteen-second videos on their social media platforms.

downloaded 1.7 billion times before being purchased by Facebook for $1 billion.

CHECK IT OUT Monetization companies use in-app advertising to maximize your mobile earnings. While they offer low cost-per-thousand impressions (CPM) rates, monetization companies bring recognition to new apps. Besides AdMob, there are a number of other mobile ad networks in the industry, each with its own packages and payment structures. These include AdWhirl, iAd, InMobi, Jumptap, Millennial Media, Mojiva, StartApp, and Tapjoy.

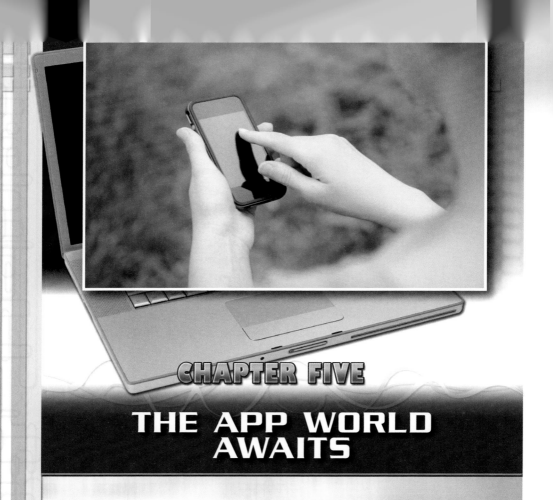

CHAPTER FIVE

THE APP WORLD AWAITS

Twenty years ago, the most established form of communication was the home phone. It was a landline, and its only features consisted of call waiting or voicemail. Today, millions of people rely on their mobile phones to not only communicate with others, but also to access information from online consulting as part of their job to ordering a large pepperoni pizza with extra cheese. Entertainment, business, pop culture, and retail are just some of the options available, thanks to an ever-changing mobile app market. Because of this, highly qualified and passionate developers are needed more than ever before.

 Landlines may soon be obsolete, as smartphones and tablets have become the popular choice for person-to-person connections. Users can freely reach out to personal and professional networks at any time and from anywhere.

 Schools.com offers an online education for those interested in turning their app development interests into a lasting career.

Starting a Career

Teen app developers face many options once they graduate from high school. Some decide to use their developing experiences as building blocks for college applications. They may want to develop skills with university studies

in computer science or software engineering. Because public and private universities are looking for well-rounded students, admissions staff look favorably on a developer's ability to be well balanced, take initiative, and participate in extracurricular activities. You want to stand out, and learning how to develop mobile apps is a good way to do that. If you have an interest and talent in development, then jump in and start developing. Release several apps in various genres to demonstrate your range. Your apps can be simple, but they also need to be in tip-top shape without errors or rough edges. Maintain a portfolio to show college recruiters what you can do. They will be impressed with the other important skills you will gain as a result of app development: professionalism, problem solving, accountability, adaptability, focus, communication skills, and self-motivation. Many schools have already begun offering specialized courses, certification, or degrees in mobile app development. Some employers require this type of experience in order to work for them as a full-time mobile app developer.

Some mobile app developers choose to skip college altogether. They may choose to take a more adventurous path toward a digital career by turning their hobby into a rewarding profession. There are endless career paths for developers, including account managers, full-time developers, consultants, software engineers, product and project managers, and quality assurance testers. As a developer with experience in the field— user interface design, computing, programming, and business expertise—you can step into one of these exciting professions. Of course, you can start your own mobile

 In 2008, venture capitalist John Doerr introduced the $100 million iFund. It was intended to appeal to developers, encouraging them to create mobile apps for the iPhone.

development company and become a member of a growing industry of appreneurs. Owning an app development business can be exciting, but it will take a great deal of dedication, time, and energy. Start-up money can help the company get off the ground, and this can either come from your own savings account or from a group of investors. If you want your company to grow quickly, it's important to have key people in place who are familiar with your preferred platform and understand complimentary aspects of mobile app development. Appreneurs can also venture into helping other developers with even greater efforts. One such company is Parse. It offers a number of services, including quick and efficient app design and server maintenance and infrastructure support

GOING GLOBAL

When you submit your app to an app store, you will be asked for particular information, including distribution. Think big. The app market is so much greater than that of your home country. China is a quickly growing market and is expected to surpass the United States in money spent on technology. New carriers are starting to distribute smartphones, meaning more subscribers could have access to your app. Even if you think your app applies to only a certain group of people in one particular geographical niche, you may be surprised. Set your app release to global distribution and watch how it attracts a number of international users. They may discover how fun and handy your new creation is and want to download it immediately.

In order to achieve this kind of exposure, consider translating your app into other languages. Mandarin and Spanish are among the most common languages spoken in the world. French, German, Italian, Portuguese, Russian, Bengali, Hindustani, and Arabic could be other options to expand your market. Professional translators can help you transfer your scripts to grammatically correct international languages. Some developers release their apps in countries smaller than their own. These markets allow them to test apps before releasing them in their homeland. Keep in mind, too, that there may be legal limitations such as content rights in other countries. Be sure to be thorough in your market research to avoid any legal issues.

for thousands of mobile applications. The Parse team knows that it's not easy to build an app, so it customized its services to provide data storage, social media integration, and push notifications alerting users of upcoming activities.

The Job Market

Because the demand for app developers is high, salaries and benefits are competitive. Sam Laird of Mashable.com notes that "the average annual salary for employed app developers in 2011 was nearly $90,000, according to one survey. And by 2016, the total revenue from consumer mobile apps is expected to top $50 billion, according to some estimates." This means that mobile app developers not only have a promising career ahead of them, but if they stay on the cutting edge of technology and creativity, they will also bring in a sizable income. Other benefits can include flexible schedules, freedom to make decisions that affect them, and entrepreneurial know-how to start their own businesses.

Whether you are a new or experienced developer, join a network within the industry. A shared interest among like-minded professionals will promote excitement and creativity while establishing resources for future projects. You can do this using online chat rooms or social media forums, or by attending annual regional and national conferences, such as the Apple Worldwide Developers Conference (WWDC). International iOS app makers are invited to attend the conference to learn about upcoming trends and cutting-edge technology. For years, participants had to be at least eighteen years of age.

Apple's developer conference, WWDC 2012, presented an in-depth look at what's new and exciting in the industry. With jam-packed sessions and hands-on labs, developers were able to stay on the cutting edge of technological trends.

However, Apple rethought this restriction after receiving numerous requests from younger developers who had a number of apps in the App Store. In June 2012, the Worldwide Developers Conference welcomed twelve- to seventeen-year-old app makers. As a result, several hundred teens and college-age students traveled to San Francisco to learn more about their industry.

If you want to travel beyond your borders, consider the Mobile World Congress (MWC). This annual event, perhaps the largest of its kind in the world, is held in Barcelona, Spain. It features keynote addresses, expert discussions, and exhibits—in English—for techies of all genres. In 2012, the Mobile World Congress had nearly seventy thousand attendees with over twelve thousand mobile app developers in attendance. Not only does the Mobile World Congress make networking easy among peers, but you may also meet your next developing partner, investor, mentor, or employer. In 2012, over 3,500 chief executive officers (CEOs) came to this worldwide event.

In the world of technology, anything is possible. The opportunities to be a part of the next big idea could be yours. Just think, you could create gesture-based interfaces, wearable computers, smart machines, or virtual worlds. Your creation could talk with users or act as a tour guide in a national park. Twenty years from now, mobile device users may look back at what passed for a smartphone and be amazed by the technological advances, all because of the contributions of people like you. Strike the mobile app market while it's hot, and learn all you can about the foundations of a solid design. These skills will eventually transfer to other technologies that could change our world. All you need is a groundbreaking idea backed up by passion, motivation, commitment, and a hunger to create something beneficial in a digital world.

QUICK TIP A number of universities now offer mobile application development degrees and certificates. They include Bryant & Stratton College Online, Full Sail University, Rasmussen College, San Diego State University, UCSD Extension, Digital Arts Center, and Walden University.

GLOSSARY

algorithm A piece of automated code used to solve a problem.

app store An online store that offers apps to buy and download for a mobile device.

branding The common theme of an organization often shown in marketing and advertising campaigns.

cross-platform formatting When an application can run on two or more mobile device platforms.

database management An assortment of programs that control the storage, modification, and extraction of data from a database.

entrepreneur One who starts and manages a business in order to make a profit.

hardware interaction A structure used to connect two devices together.

memory allocation The process by which a specific amount of memory space is reserved for programs or services on a mobile device or computer.

monetization partner A person who generates revenue using affiliate advertising, content, or programs within a blog, Web site, or mobile app.

nag screen A pop-up reminder that alerts users to paid versions of an app.

network A system that spreads data between users. It includes the operating system, connecting cables, antennas, towers, and supporting hardware.

operating system A system that provides a user interface between a mobile app and computer hardware.

platform The operating system of a mobile device.

revenue A substantial amount of money earned by a company or organization.

server-side language A technique used to embed scripts in an HTML source code resulting in information being processed by a script running server-side.

software Programming code that provides performance instructions to hardware.

software development kit A set of program tools that allows a developer to create mobile apps.

user interface (UI) The system in which the user engages with a mobile device. The UI includes the aesthetic appearance, onscreen menu system, response time, and content of the device.

Web application framework A software structure that supports Web app development, as well as the creation of Web sites, services, and resources.

FOR MORE INFORMATION

Apple Worldwide Developer Conference
1 Infinite Loop
Cupertino, CA 95014
(800) 676-2775 in the United States
(800) 692-7753 in Canada
Web site: https://developer.apple.com/wwdc
Since 1983, the Apple Worldwide Developers Conference
    (WWDC) has been showcasing Apple's newest soft-
    ware and technologies. Developers from all over
    the world attend to participate in various hands-on
    sessions and network with other developers.

News Corporation
1211 Avenue of the Americas
New York, NY 10036
(212) 852-7000
Web site: http://www.newscorp.com
One of the world's largest media groups, News Corporation
    has holdings in film, music, radio, television, maga-
    zines, newspapers, and publishing.

Schools.com
QuinStreet, Inc.
950 Tower Lane, 6th Floor
Foster City, CA 94404
Web site: http://www.schools.com
Schools.com helps students explore local and global
    options for accredited universities and online

schools. It offers tools, information, and contacts to fit educational goals.

TED Conferences LLC
250 Hudson Street, Suite 1002
New York, NY 10013
(212) 346-9333
Web site: http://www.ted.com
Since 1984, TED has been sharing "ideas worth spreading" with the help of experts in technology, entertainment, and design.

World Mobile Congress
GSMA Head Office, 7th Floor
5 New Street Square
New Fetter Lane
London, EC4A 3BF
England
Web site: http://www.mobileworldcongress.com
World Mobile Congress is the world's largest mobile event featuring keynote speakers, panel discussions, exhibitions, and new technology. Since 1987, techies have been traveling to the annual conference to make deals and seek industry and networking opportunities.

Yahoo! Inc.
701 First Avenue
Sunnyvale, CA 94089
(408) 349-3300
Web site: http://www.yahoo.com

Founded in 1995 by Jerry Yang and David Filo, Yahoo! is
an online commerce and media company serving
over 345 million customers a month. Yahoo! also
offers advertising, business, household, and online
services.

Yahoo! Inc. Canada
207 Queens Quay W
Toronto, ON M5J 1A7
Canada
(416) 341-8605
Web site: http://www.yahoo.com
Yahoo! is a global Web network with offices in Canada,
Australia, and the United States, as well as Europe,
Asia, and Latin America.

Web Sites

Due to the changing nature of Internet links, Rosen
Publishing has developed an online list of Web sites
related to the subject of this book. This site is updated regu-
larly. Please use this link to access the list:

http://www.rosenlinks.com/DCB/CMA

FOR FURTHER READING

Anderson, Stephen P. *Seductive Interaction Design: Creating Playful, Fun, and Effective User Experiences* (Voices That Matter). Berkeley, CA: New Riders, 2011.

Branson, Richard. *Like a Virgin: Secrets They Won't Teach You at Business School*. New York, NY: Penguin Group, 2012.

Burd, Barry. *Beginning Programming with Java for Dummies*. Hoboken, NJ: Wiley Publishing, Inc., 2012.

Burton, Michael, and Donn Felker. *Android Application Development for Dummies*. Hoboken, NJ: Wiley Publishing, Inc., 2012.

Daley, Michael. *Learning iOS Game Programming: A Hands-On Guide to Building Your First iPhone Game*. Boston, MA: Pearson Education, Inc., 2011.

DeMarco, M. J. *The Millionaire Fastlane: Crack the Code to Wealth and Live Rich for a Lifetime*. Phoenix, AZ: Viperion Publishing Corporation, 2011.

Goldstein, Neal. *iPad Application Development for Dummies*. Hoboken, NJ: Wiley Publishing, Inc., 2012.

Goldstein, Neal. *iPhone Application Development for Dummies*. Hoboken, NJ: Wiley Publishing, Inc., 2009.

Goldstein, Neal. *Objective-C Programming for Dummies*. Hoboken, NJ: Wiley Publishing, Inc., 2012.

Goldstein, Neal, and Dave Wilson. *iOS 6 Application Development for Dummies*. Hoboken, NJ: Wiley Publishing, Inc., 2013.

Lee, Shane. *The App Store Playbook: Discover How 10 Successful iPhone App Developers Hit It Big Selling Games on the App Store*. Seattle, WA: CreateSpace Independent Publishing Platform, 2012.

McWherter, Jeff, and Scott Gowell. *Professional Mobile Application Development*. Hoboken, NJ: Wrox, 2012.

Mureta, Chad. *App Empire: Make Money, Have a Life, and Let Technology Work for You*. Hoboken, NJ: Wiley Publishing, Inc., 2012.

Neil, Theresa. *Mobile Design Pattern Gallery: UI Patterns for Mobile Applications*. Sebastopol, CA: O'Reilly Media, Inc., 2012.

O'Rourke, Jodie. *Flash Mobile Application Development for Dummies*. Hoboken, NJ: Wiley Publishing, Inc., 2011.

Pierce, Taylor A. *Appreneur—Secrets to Success in the App Store*. Seattle, WA: CreateSpace Independent Publishing Platform, 2012.

Warner, Janine, and David LaFontaine. *Mobile Web Design for Dummies*. Hoboken, NJ: Wiley Publishing, Inc., 2010.

Welch, Shawn. *From Idea to App: Creating iOS UI, Animations, and Gestures (*Voices That Matter*)*. Berkeley, CA: New Riders, 2011.

Yarmosh, Ken. *App Savvy: Turning Ideas into iPad and iPhone Apps Customers Really Want*. Sebastopol, CA: O'Reilly Media, Inc., 2010.

Zechner, Mario. *Beginning Android Games*. New York, NY: Apress Media, LLC, 2011.

BIBLIOGRAPHY

Brin, Dinah Wisenberg. "The New Cool Kids: Teenage-App Developers." Young Entrepreneur, 2013. Retrieved March 20, 2013 (http://www. youngentrepreneur.com/startingup/start-ups /the-new-cool-kids-teenage-app-developers).

Chen, Brian X. "iPhone Developers Go from Rags to Riches." *Wired*, 2008. Retrieved April 1, 2013 (http://www.wired.com/gadgetlab/2008/09/indie-developer).

Costanzo, Spencer. "My First Apps: Tips for New App Developers." 2012. Retrieved March 20, 2013 (http://www.spencercostanzo.com/2/post/2012/12 /my-first-apps-tips-for-new-app-developers.html).

Ellin, Abby, and Joanna Stern. "12-Year-Old App Developer Wins Award." ABCNews.com, 2012. Retrieved March 20, 2013 (http://abcnews.go .com/Technology/12-year-california-app-developer-wins-award/story?id = 16230236#.UOegMGnnbIW).

Entertainment Software Association. "The Evolution of Mobile Games." Retrieved April 1, 2013 (http:// www.theesa.com/games-improving-what-matters /mobile-games.asp).

Ferriss, Tim. "How to Build an App Empire: Can You Create the Next Instagram?" The 4-Hour Workweek, 2012. Retrieved March 20, 2013 (http://www.fourhourworkweek.com/blog/2012/04 /22/how-to-build-an-app-empire-can-you-create-the -next-instagram).

Grandoni, Dino. "17-Year-Old Summly Founder Nick D'Aloisio's Immodest Goal: Change the Way You Read News." *Huffington Post*, 2012. Retrieved March 20, 2013 (http://www.huffingtonpost.com/2012/11/02/summly-nick-daloisio_n_2065796.html).

Kooser, Amanda. "Meet Connor, a 7-Year-Old iPhone App Developer." Cnet.com, 2011. Retrieved March 1, 2013 (http://news.cnet.com/8301-17938_105-20093715-1/meet-connor-a-7-year-old-iphone-app-developer).

Manoogian, John, III. "How Free Apps Can Make More Money Than Paid Apps." Techcrunch.com, 2012. Retrieved March 1, 2013 (http://techcrunch.com/2012/08/26/how-free-apps-can-make-more-money-than-paid-apps).

Marino, Kristin. "How to Become a Mobile App Developer." Schools.com, 2012. Retrieved April 1, 2013 (http://www.schools.com/visuals/how-to-become-mobile-app-developer.html).

Michael, Sarah, and AFP. "Yahoo! Buys App Summly from Australian-British Inventor Nick D'Aloisio, 17." News.com.au, 2013. Retrieved April 1, 2013 (http://www.news.com.au/technology/yahoo-buys-app-from-teen-inventor/story-e6frfro0-1226605913738#ixzz2PFpOWJSn).

Mobile Tuxedo. "8 Ways to Make Profit with Free Mobile Apps." 2012. Retrieved April 1, 2013. (http://www.mobiletuxedo.com/8-ways-to-make-profit-with-free-mobile-apps).

mobiThinking. "Global Mobile Statistics 2012 Part E: Mobile Apps, App Stores, Pricing and Failure Rates." 2012. Retrieved April 1, 2013 (http://mobithinking .mobi/mobile-marketing-tools/latest-mobile-stats/e).

Ohngren, Kara. "How One Teenage Trep Snubbed College to Build an Apps Empire." Young Entrepreneur, 2012. Retrieved February 23, 2013 (http://www.youngentrepreneur.com/startingup/st art-ups/how-one-teenage-trep-snubbed-college-to- build-an-apps-empire).

Parmar, Neil. "3 Ways to Outfox the Apps Craze." Young Entrepreneur, 2012. Retrieved March 20, 2013 (http://www.youngentrepreneur.com/startingup /marketing-strategies/3-ways-to-outfox-the-apps -craze).

Rooney, Ben. "What Does $30 Million Buy You?" *Wall Street Journal*, March 26, 2013. Retrieved April 1, 2013 (http://blogs.wsj.com/tech-europe/2013/03 /26/what-does-30-million-buy-you/?mod = WSJ _article_outbrain&obref = obinsite).

TED Talks. "Thomas Suarez: A 12-Year-Old App Developer." 2011. Retrieved April 1, 2013 (http:// www.ted.com/talks/thomas_suarez_a_12_year_old_ app_developer.html).

INDEX

About the Author

Erin Staley's work ranges from nonfiction books (Rosen Publishing) to cocreating and cofacilitating writer workshops with her critique partner. She lives in Mexico.

Photo Credits

Cover, p. 1 (icons), p. 14 (inset) © iStockphoto.com/scanrail; cover, pp. 1, 4, 14, 25, 34, 44 (laptop) © iStockphoto.com/Lisa Thornberg; cover, p. 1 (smartphone) © iStockphoto.com /cotesebastien; cover, interior pages (mouse) © iStockphoto .com/abu; p. 4 (inset) © iStockphoto.com/hanibaram; p. 5 svetikd/E+/Getty Images; pp. 7, 35, 38–39 Bloomberg /Getty Images; pp. 11, 32 © AP Images; p. 15 Ethan Miller/Getty Images; p. 19 Rex Features/AP Images; p. 21 Jemal Countess/Getty Images; p. 25 (inset) © iStockphoto .com/vitchanan; p. 26 Mark Bowden/E+/Getty Images; p. 28 © RumbleApps; p. 30 Jonathan Nackstrand/AFP/Getty Images; p. 34 (inset) © iStockphoto.com/Leontura; p. 42 Press Association/AP Images; p. 44 (inset) © iStockphoto.com /Anatoliy Babiy; p. 45 Stockbyte/Thinkstock; p. 47 David Paul Morris/Getty Images; p. 50 AFP/Getty Images; cover and interior pages background patterns and graphics © iStockphoto.com/Ali Mazraie Shadi, © iStockphoto.com /MISHA, © iStockphoto.com/Paul Hill, © iStockphoto.com /Charles Taylor, © iStockphoto.com/Daniel Halvorson, © iStockphoto.com/Jeffrey Sheldon.

Designer: Nicole Russo, Editor: Bethany Bryan
Researcher: Marty Levick